# Secrets of Fast Growth in Catfish

# Secrets of Fast Growth in Catfish

A revelation on how big-sized table fish can be produced in just 4 months thereby achieving three production cycles in a year

Anthony Adefarakan

AQUATON KONSULTS

# CONTENTS

INTRODUCTION

ENEMIES OF GOOD GROWTH IN CATFISH

SECRETS OF FAST GROWTH IN CATFISH

ABOUT THE AUTHOR

# A NOTE FROM EL-ADONAI: THE CHAIRMAN OF AQUATON KONSULTS

Beloved Reader,

You are highly favored and enviably blessed to have a copy of this handbook in your hands at this moment, because all you will read therein are products of My inspiration.

As far back as Genesis 1:20-22, on the fifth day of My creation work, I commanded the waters to bring forth fishes of every kind, and they all came to being at My command.

And because they came at My command, all their activities – feeding, breathing, swimming, reproduction, growth etc – are regulated by Me. As their Creator, I determine which one survives or not, which one grows well or not among other outcomes of their existence (Ps. 115:3).

I am so interested in fishes, and I demonstrated this in the ministry of My Son – Jesus Christ – when He was with you on earth. For instance;

1. In Matt. 4:18-22, the first disciples I chose for Him were fishermen (fish dealers).
2. In John 6:5-13, He fed the 5,000 with five loaves of bread and two fishes.
3. In Matt 15:32-38, He fed the 4,000 with seven loaves of bread and few little fishes.
4. In Matt 17:24-27, I sent Him money through a fish to pay His tax.

5. In John 21:5-6, He gave His disciples abundant harvest of fishes.
6. In John 21:9-13, He cooked fish for His disciples to eat.
7. In Matt. 4:19, He termed soul winning as "fishing for men's souls".
8. In Luke 5:1-11, He filled Peter's net with fishes until his boat began to sink.

It therefore implies that for you to succeed in this your fisheries project, you really need the help of My Son – **Jesus Christ** – who knows so much about fishes. I will recommend you accept His Lordship over your life and the project so that He can show you the way to succeed. Remember, "Without Him, you can do nothing" (John 15:5). Tell Him these if you want Him to help you: *"Dear Lord Jesus, I give my life to you as my Lord and Savior so that you will help me. Lord Jesus, I dedicate my spirit, soul, body and this fisheries project to you; help me and guide me. Thank you for saving me. Now, my success is guaranteed in Jesus' Name. Amen".*

Congratulations! Now go ahead, read the manual and apply the principles written therein, your success is guaranteed. All the best!

*With love from:*
**El-Adonai,**
*Chairman, Aquaton Konsults*

# INTRODUCTION

Catfish farming has in recent years become one of the fastest growing ventures around the world, even as professionals, civil servants, businessmen, business women, clergymen among other people in different professions are now engaging in the practice both at subsistence and commercial levels.

The awareness is so great that an average investor wants to commit some capital into this aspect of agriculture; and the rate of consumption of these catfish is so high that demand sometimes exceeds supply. This wide acceptance is largely due to its unique taste and health advantage over red meat as declared by doctors (nutritionists). However, most farmers are faced with one challenge or the other in the culture process, and one of such major areas of concern is the issue of producing stunted, small-sized table fish at harvest period. Some farmers stock their ponds and six months later, they are still struggling to achieve one kilogram (1kg) of table fish. This is not normal. And the reason for this most times is the farmers' inadequate knowledge on how catfish should be cultured and raised. There are certain keys meant for certain doors without which the doors will remain shut. Also, for catfish, there are certain keys needed to unlock their growth potentials in such a way that in four (4) months, you will be producing big sized table fish without struggle, thereby enabling you to achieve three (3) cycles of production in a 12 months calendar year.

What you are about to encounter in this handbook are the secrets you need to know and apply in order to get your desired results in catfish farming. Read carefully and pick the keys.

# ENEMIES OF GOOD GROWTH IN CATFISH

These refer to the causes of stunted growth, and wrong practices in catfish culture which are capable of turning the entire venture into a failure. They are highlighted as follows:

## 2.1 Poor Fish Seeds

Fish seeds are the fingerlings or juveniles produced or procured and stocked in order for them to grow into table fish. However, they could be viable or poor. Poor seeds result from bad, immature parent stocks (broodstocks), wrong hatchery practices, improper fish treatment during crisis, runts selection among others.

Now, stocking such poor seeds has already set the pace for failure and you can be sure you will struggle raising them to your desired size. Poor fish seeds are therefore the non-performing or low performing seeds.

## 2.2 Wrong Stocking Density – Overstocking

Stocking a pond without determining its stocking capacity is gambling. When a pond is overstocked, there will definitely be overcrowding which researches have shown to be capable of resulting in stunted growth, disease transfer, stiff competition for feed, cannibalism among other detrimental consequences. This overstocking is one of the major hindrances to good growth in catfish.

## 2.3 Poor Water Quality

Most farmers have erroneously assumed that once their water is clean and crystal clear, it is good for catfish culture without taking the chemistry of such water into consideration. Stocking fish in ponds containing water with poor parameters is a sure way to failure, especially when the pH is not suitable. There is no way catfish will grow optimally under poor water quality condition.

## 2.4 Poor Feeds and Feeding

Poor quality feeds – with insufficient crude protein levels, fibre contents, among other vital nutrients will always lead to poor growth. Catfish grows in proportion to the feed it is fed with, thus poor feed will definitely result in poor growth. Aside insufficient nutrients in the feed, some of these feeds may also have expired, grown moulds and even fermented. Feeding such feeds to the fish will yield nothing but poor results. Also, some farmers have been discovered to be feeding things like garri, bread, rice etc to their fish stocks, hiding under the fact that the fish are eating them. Well, hunger makes anything look like feed and when the preferable is not available, the available becomes preferable, and that's why they've been eating it, but never expect them to achieve your desired growth with such menu.

On the other hand, poor feeding methods and regimes like once in a day feeding, twice in a week feeding and pouring of feed over the water surface without waiting to check the fish's response are all wrong practices that will prevent your desired yield. Even when the quality of their feed is good, poor methods of feeding/poor feeding regimes will still result in poor growth. Many farmers have failed mainly due to these factors.

## 2.5 Erratic Culture Practices – Inconsistency in Manage-ment Practices

This refers to the failure on the part of the farmers to maintain consistent culture practices, and most of the management practices are in the form of routines. When a farmer changes the fish's water only when he remembers, feeds only when it's convenient, sorts only when he feels like and doesn't bother to consistently check the status of the water parameters – poor growth will be the inevitable result. This is because the habitat condition will be altered which may likely make the fish susceptible to infections, and sure enough, when fish are sick or their habitat is not conducive, proper growth becomes a mirage.

### 2.6 Oxygen Depletion

When there is depletion or insufficient oxygen in the culture water, the fish are bound to experience crisis. No animal can survive when oxygen is lacking; thus when this happens, the fish are struggling and "thinking" of how to survive not how they will grow. Under this life threatening condition – which mostly occur due to unchecked ammonia build up in the culture system as well as uncontrolled algae bloom, their activities such as feeding, respiration, swimming etc will be impaired and that's why they most times resolve to hanging in order to engage their accessory breathing organs. Now, you can be sure while all these are going on, there can't be anything called meaningful growth.

### 2.7 Failure to Sort/Improper Sorting

Some farmers have been discovered to just stock their ponds with fish and leave them like that till harvest time without sorting; this is a very wrong practice. Even some who claim to sort do so ineffectively. Probably due to the work involved, they just do some picking and dropping here and there and call it sorting. Failure to sort or improper sorting will lead to stiff competition for food, cannibalism, frequent oxygen depletion, frequent ammonia build up etc and these are inhibitors to proper growth in catfish. Most times when sorting is not done, you notice one or two fish becoming very big while others remain stunted. That's the way it is. Others would have been like those two if sorting was properly done.

## 2.8 Infection or Diseases – Wrong Treatment and Treatment Methods

In the culture process there are likelihoods of infections or diseases - which from experience are discovered to be mostly caused by wrong management practices as catfish hardly become sick. However, when this occurs, there can't be growth – a sick fish doesn't grow. And in treating the fish, wrong treatment and treatment methods without the guidance of an expert will likely worsen the condition or even make it spread to the initially unaffected stocks. Wrong treatment of catfish can lead to death, not even talking about growth now. This is because there are certain doses of fish drugs that can heal; at wrong doses, they can kill the fish.

## 2.9 Wrong Pond Management Practices

Proper pond management cannot be overemphasized in achieving the desired result. Not taking care of these ponds where the fish are expected to live and grow will spell failure. Not sanitizing the pond periodically, not treating the pond itself, not protecting the pond against pollution, etc will hinder the manifestation of the expected results. Some of these ponds have become hosts to pathogens – disease causing microorganisms; thus treating the fish without taking care of the pond containing the fish is like cutting off the branches of a tree without uprooting the tree itself, it is a matter of time, the branches will grow again. Some farmers complain, 'I've treated my fish and they are still not fine'; may be unknown to them, it's actually the pond that needs to be treated. The pond must be conducive to support proper fish growth, or else, other efforts toward good growth will be frustrated.

## 2.10 Engagement of Wrong Consultancy Services

Honestly speaking, many farmers would have succeeded but for wrong counsels from these so called 'consultants'. Taking advice from non-professionals parading themselves as consultants has a lot to do with the final outcome of the venture. Gullibly believing these quacks may lead to wrong pond constructions, improper stocking density, production of runts as fish seeds, poor water quality, poor feeding methods etc; and there's no way good growth will be achieved when one or two of these wrong factors are present. It might interest you to know that good growths of catfish are not achieved in some farms singularly due to wrong consultancy services. Once the right conditions are not provided, good growth in catfish simply becomes wishful thinking.

# SECRETS OF FAST GROWTH IN CATFISH

As earlier mentioned in the introduction; the keys being made available to you in this session represent the secrets of achieving fast growth in catfish. These principles are not to be separated from one another; it is practicing them in totality that guarantees your desired results regardless of the system you are into – be it earthen ponds, concrete ponds or even tarpaulin ponds. They are as follows:

### 3.1 Good Fish Seeds

The importance of stocking good and viable fish seeds cannot be overemphasized in laying a good foundation for fast growth. Fish seeds range from frys to fingerlings and to juveniles. Fingerlings are the seeds between 4 – 5 weeks old while juveniles are those between 8 – 10 weeks old. Now, I've always told my customers, and those who have been complying have not had any cause to regret. Stocking fingerlings is not as safe as stocking juveniles. Fingerlings are tenderer compared to juveniles, and as a matter of fact, there are still some nursery works – including treatments, to be done on fingerlings before they can withstand outdoor stocking conditions. And that's why the mortality rate is higher in them – due to water parameters fluctuations, handling stress, among other life threatening conditions – compared to juveniles which are more hardy and tolerant to these same conditions.

You are advised to procure and stock juveniles – fish seeds of not less than 8 weeks old and you'll be on your way to recording your desired result. It is more difficult to raise fingerlings than to raise juveniles. Though the cost is higher, yet it is still the better option. And if you're into breeding, ensure you get good broodstocks and carry out all the required hatchery and nursery practices in order to raise formidable fish seeds. (You can get a copy of my handbook **Catfish Breeding** for details on the required practices). Don't take the fish out for stocking until they are juveniles; that is a good way of laying the foundation for fast growth in catfish.

### 3.2 Correct Stocking Density

Stocking density talks about how many fish a particular pond can contain without being overstocked or under stocked. Ponds are constructed with various dimensions; and these form the basis for calculating the correct stocking density. For catfish, the correct stocking densities are as follows:

1. Stocking density for catfish to be raised in concrete and mobile tanks : 40 – 60 fish/cubic metre
2. Stocking density for catfish to be raised in earthen ponds (the closest system to the natural): 60 – 80 fish/cubic metre

**Note:** This is based on the carrying capacity of the ponds at harvest and not at the point of fish introduction into the ponds. That is, at introduction the ponds may accommodate a lot of fish but as they begin to grow, the ponds will eventually become too small for them. Thus, the stocking densities highlighted above guide on the population of stock a particular tank or pond can produce per production batch.
(These can also be slightly manipulated depending on the farmer's management skills).
However, in recirculatory systems, the stocking density is always higher. It can be between 200 – 300 fish/cubic metre, being an intensive culture system.

To calculate the numbers of fish that can be stocked in a particular pond; follow these steps;

- Take the dimension of the pond (length, breadth and depth) in metres.
- Multiply the dimension, (l x b x depth) and your result will be in m$^3$
- Then multiply the answer by the number of fish required to be stocked per cubic metre (as written above)
- Your final result is the number of fish to be stocked and produced in that pond.

For example, in a concrete pond of dimension 6m x 4m x 1.5m which is equivalent to 36m$^3$, you multiply 36m$^3$ x 40 fish which is equal to 1,440 fish. Therefore, in that pond with dimension 6m x 4m x 1.5m, 1,440 fish will be its correct stocking density i.e. the number of fish to be stocked and produced in it is 1,440. The same applies for other culture systems. When ponds are correctly stocked, good growth is inevitable because space contributes immensely to catfish's fast growth.

### 3.3 Good Water Quality

Catfish, like every other kind of fishes, are aquatic organisms, and all their activities like respiration, reproduction, locomotion, nutrition, excretion etc take place in the water. With this understanding, it becomes expedient to know the kind of water qualities/parameters that can sustain catfish and as a result enhance their fast growth.

Firstly, it is important to note that not all clean water are good water for catfish. The water may be clean and deadly. A major water quality parameter worth considering in this regard is the pH – which is a measure of the alkaline and acid content of water given by the level of hydrogen ion ($H^+$) dissolved in the water. It is measured with a pH meter graduated from 0 – 14, with 6.5 – 7.5 as a measure of neutrality, while 0 – 6.4 is the measure of water acidity and 7.6 – 14 is the measure of water alkalinity.

Note this, a slightly acidic water may not be lethal i.e. it may not kill the fish, but it will prevent good growth. However, when the level of acidity is so high, say like 4.0 or 3.0, it may lead to mortality, especially at juveniles stage.

Now, for good and fast growth of your stock, test the water you intend stocking in using a pH meter – you may call us to do this test for you. The required pH range for the growth you expect to record is between 6.5 – 8.0. Catfish will grow rapidly under this pH condition because feed will be optimally utilized and converted to flesh; there'll be resistance to diseases, and the water medium will be conducive for other activities to be carried out by the fish.

However, if your water doesn't fall within the range; there is what to do. If it falls below 6.5, it is acidic and to still make use of that same water, you will have to boost it with liming materials like soda ash, bicarbonate of soda, agricultural lime, slaked lime, quicklime, calcium cyanide etc, with their dosages depending on the level of acidity. You will need the help of an expert to apply these materials correctly in order to bring your water to the appropriate pH range. If on the other hand, your water shoots beyond 8.0, it is alkaline. $AlSO_4$ (alum) will be needed to lower it by decreasing the total concentration of basic minerals in the water. You will as well need the help of an expert in administering this.

Under a good pH condition (with other factors in place); catfish has no other option than to grow rapidly. pH is not the only water parameter that must be made good; others like temperature with a conducive range of $27^0c$ – $30^0c$, ammonia level, $CO_2$, turbidity etc should be adequately regulated for optimum performance of the catfish. But before all these are considered, the pH must be conducive. It is a MUST.

### 3.4 Good Feed and Correct Feeding Regimes

Catfish grows only by converting feed fed to flesh - under appropriate culture conditions. In catfish, it is "no feed, no growth";

"poor feed, poor growth". Good feeds are the feeds with the catfish's required level of nutrient. For instance, catfish that is expected to growth rapidly in four months shouldn't be fed with any feed containing less than 40% crude protein (CP). Other nutrients are of importance as well, but the CP level must be carefully considered or worked out if local formulation is being done. Another factor is fish's acceptance of the feed. Some farmers use certain feed types because others are using them, it is not totally correct. If your fish responds well, good; but if not, you'll have to change to what your fish accepts, having in mind that until they eat the feed, there's not going to be any conversion to flesh, which is what results in good weight. Another aspect you must take note of is feeding the fish with the correct size of feed at certain stages of their growth. Feeding 4.5mm feed to juveniles for instance is improper, their mouth can only take 2mm – 3mm so you must know what size they're to take at each stage of their growth. (You can pick a copy of my handbook **A Detailed Handbook on Fish Production** for details on when and how feed sizes can be switched).

Now, to feeding methods and feeding regimes, care must be taken to ensure these are correctly done. There are two main methods of feeding employed in catfish farming. Feeding by body weight and discretional feeding which can be administered either by broadcast or spot feeding. To feed by body weight, you will have to carry out sampling and do some calculations to know what a particular fish size can be fed with (this is also explained in details in the book referred to above). On the other hand, discretional feeding is done by feeding the fish until they stop feeding at each regime. When they stop eating, you stop feeding, or else the water will be polluted by uneaten feed. Employing broadcast feeding is spreading a quantity of feed across the water from end to end, expecting the fish to come up to eat them, while spot feeding has to do with establishing a particular spot in the pond where you stand to feed them, and they in turn will always come to that spot to feed whenever it is feeding time.

Either of the methods could be employed, the most important thing is just to ensure that the fish are actually eating the feed.

Feeding regimes talk about the periods of feeding. Catfish have short intestines and as a result, they're quickly filled when eating, just that they'll soon digest the feed and come back for more. In the light of this, you can establish a three-four hours intervals for feeding them. For instance, you may establish 7am, 10am, 1pm, 4pm, 7pm or 8am, 12pm, 4pm, 8pm as feeding regimes for your stock depending on your schedule. But once a particular regime is established, do all in your power to be consistent because the fish are disciplined enough to expect to be fed at the established regimes.

With all these in place, your catfish cannot escape fast growth in four months.

### 3.5 Consistent Culture Practices

Catfish farming requires discipline. Most of the management practices are routines, but they must be consistently adhered to for good result. Take for instance, if for the first two months of your culture, you maintain a good water pH, good feeding at the established regimes and so on, then suddenly in the third month, you stop maintaining your water quality, start feeding whenever you remember, among other erratic culture practices, you have literally signed in for failure. Catfish need consistent culture practices to grow fast. Any alteration in their condition will hinder their optimum performance. It is just like the Biblical example of laying one's hand on the plow without looking back. Once you decide to go into catfish production, you must be willing and ready to give it all it takes to succeed – on a consistent basis. Also, this consistency finds application in production cycles. If you carried out certain practices that delivered your expected results in four months, what stops you from doing same or even better in the subsequent productions? Many farmers get carried away by their success in a cycle and fail to engage the same principles in the following cycles; this is inconsistency. Once you have the keys to fast growth, you should never have slow growth again – if only you will be willing to apply the keys in your production cycles. Thus consistent culture practices – doing the right thing on a regular basis will surely enhance the fast growth you desire.

### 3.6 Oxygen Availability

Aquatic animals make use of what is called dissolved oxygen; and since catfish is one of those animals, it uses the same. The oxygen has to be in dissolved form in water because they respire through gill exchange. There are instruments used to measure the oxygen levels in water, but you don't have to, since there are other means you can employ.

Practically speaking now, when the level of the dissolved oxygen in your water is adequate, your catfish will go down i.e they will make use of your pond bottom, but when it is inadequate, you'll see them coming up, standing erect in order to tap some atmospheric oxygen. When you observe this, it's an indication that the dissolved oxygen in their water has been used up and needs to be replenished. If you don't quickly attend to this, they'll become stressed and vulnerable to any unhealthy conditions. To make oxygen available in the pond water, you may make use of aerators which generate oxygen molecules in the water. On the other hand, you may agitate the water by opening your inlet tap, which works best with perforated pipes. As the water drops in, fresh oxygen is made available to the fish. When the situation is very bad, you may have to change the water with a totally fresh one and you'll see them going down again.

Please note, when they start hanging this way, you don't feed as that will further worsen the condition. What they need under this condition is oxygen, not food. Rainfall also helps to agitate the water for more oxygen availability, just that you must watch out for overflow; and that's why an overflow pipe is always constructed with ponds.

When the sufficient dissolved oxygen is available, all other activities will go on well and good growth will be the resultant effect.

### 3.7 **Timely and Proper Sorting**

Sorting is a compulsory exercise in catfish farming. This is because they cannibalize on one another; and feed efficiency is not always guaranteed when it is not done. Sorting must be timely and correct. For instance, two - three weeks after stocking your pond, the first sorting should be carried out to check for growth differences thus preventing cannibalism. There must have been some which have outgrown others, usually not very many; they are to be taken out to a separate tank. Why? Their presence with the others will lead to reduction in your stock because they must surely feed on some of them. Also, their size will terrorize others during feeding, thus it is only after they are satisfied that the other ones will be able to feed well. But if they are on their own, there won't be any to terrorize and others too will be free to grow well.

In the $2^{nd}$ month as well, another sorting should be done. This is most appropriately referred to as grading. This time around, you completely drain the pond and grade your stock into sizes. Some may be big, medium or small. You will grade them into what your ponds can contain till harvest i.e the correct stocking density required at harvest. That's when you will know those that will be harvested first based on their potentials. You will grade them into the ponds by sizes and the results of this exercise are good spaces for fast growth, feed efficiency – as you will know which feed grade a particular size should take, drastically reduced cannibalism and informed harvest projections – as you will become aware of what to expect at harvest. This exercise must be thorough or else, its purpose will not be accomplished. To the "how", sorting should be done either early in the morning or late in the evening. It should never be done under the sun as this will constitute unbearable stress and even sun burn to the fish. And no feeding should be done before carrying out the exercise. Even after the sorting has been done, a minimum allowance of 1 hour must be given before 'light' feeding is done. (You can refer to question 11 in my handbook titled **"50 Frequently Asked Questions by Fish Farmers with De-**

tailed Answers" for more information on sorting). Timely and proper sorting will always deliver fast growth in catfish.

## 3.8 Prevention and Prompt Treatment of Infection/ Diseases

Catfish hardly get sick, especially when all the required management practices are faithfully adhered to. They are very hardy and tolerant. In fact, my customers who have faithfully adhered to my instructions on this catfish culture have never had any cause to call me to handle any crisis or disease condition for them from stocking to harvest. It is a very sweet practice once you know what to do and do it.

Also, one good thing about this practice is that you can give preventive doses of certain fish drugs to enhance their immunity.

You may do this each time you change your water or during sorting. You can as well administer some through their feed – all in a bid to prevent them from being sick (though you will need the guidance of an expert in doing this).

However, when there is an infection or a disease outbreak; you must be very observant to know at the early state, so as to quickly treat them. Once you begin to notice poor response to feeding, irregular swimming, cutting or whitish barbels (whiskers), white spots on the head, broken skulls, fin rots, cutting tails, dull movement, belly burst among other strange conditions you've not been noticing before, quickly call the attention of a fisheries expert, who will be able to decode what the symptoms mean and administer the right medication. He may not always be there in person but he'll surely guide you on what to do. Self- medication in catfish farming is dangerous, because the same drugs used in curing diseases also have the capacity to wipe out the entire stock. Care must be taken.

Please note, when your fish are sick, reduce your feeding so as not to worsen the condition by polluting their water. And in case of any death, quickly remove and bury so as to prevent a spread (in case the condition is infectious). Also, if only one pond is affected, don't use the equipment you use there for other unaffected ponds so as not to transfer the infection.

When fish is sick, growth automatically stops; and it will only resume when it becomes well again. Thus, to secure fast growth, **PREVENTION IS BETTER THAN CURE!**

### 3.9 Correct Pond Management Practices

The ponds being used in culturing these fish must be properly taken care of. This is because the growth you expect is going to happen in there and without taking good care of it, your desired result may be jeopardized.

Some of the correct pond care practices include washing the pond thoroughly with salt before stocking, ensuring there are no stones or sharp objects at the pond bottom capable of bringing injury (bruises) to the fish – which may serve as entry points to pathogens (knowing fully well that catfish are bottom dwellers), cleaning of the pond sides (walls) when water is being changed – by scrubbing off the algae deposits and rinsing with salt solution, mending any discovered cracks, ensuring the outlets are corked so as not to leak out the water overnight, proper regulation of inlets, protection with nets (wire gauze) to prevent their jumping out and getting wounded; restriction of visitors to the pond area to prevent pollution and poaching, sanitation of the pond area to keep predators away, and so on. This depends on the type of system you are into, be it earthen ponds, concrete or tarpaulin ponds. Some of the practices are relative. In any way you can, ensure your ponds and your pond area are always in good condition and there'll not be any hide out for any disease causing organisms or anything of such. This will inevitably bring about your desired fast growth.

### 3.10 Engagement of Tested and Proven Consultancy Services

This is the way I will like to approach this. A man who has never had headache surely does not know what it means to have it and he's therefore the wrong person to approach for the cure to headache. It works the same way. You can only get help from someone who knows what you are facing by experience and knowledge. Thus to succeed in this venture, make in-depth enquiries before you engage the service of any consultant. It is not enough to study fisheries as a course in school, such consultant must be a practitioner i.e a field person. This will help you a lot, because you will at one time or the other need the assistance of their expertise and it is only in getting the right person that success can be guaranteed.

All the aforementioned keys constitute secrets you need to know and apply in order to achieve fast growth in catfish within a space of 4 months. They have been tested and proven to be true. All you need do is to engage them as well and add your own story to the testimonies of others. But remember please, it takes the shell, the yolk and the albumin to have an egg. All these must be harmonized to achieve your desired fast growth.

**For any enquiries or to place orders for any of our books,**
**Email: aquatonkonsults@yahoo.com**

# ABOUT THE AUTHOR

Prince Anthony Adefarakan as he is popularly called is the M.D/CEO of Aquaton Konsults, Nigeria, West Africa. He is an experienced Fisheries Consultant with vast wealth of knowledge in matters relating to fish production. He has practically demonstrated artificial fish breeding, fish ponds construction, fish feeding, fish disease and management among other fish production techniques to a large number of farmers far and wide. In addition to training these farmers (some of which are students, retirees and investors), he has been personally involved in their business set up; providing the necessary resources to ensure their success.

At some point in his Fisheries career, he served as a Master Aquaculture Service Provider (MASP) to a Department for International Development (DFID) funded project in the Niger Delta part of Nigeria (Market Development Project in the Niger Delta). He also served as one of the USAID's Nigerian Agricultural Enterprise Curriculum (NAEC) trainers in the Niger Delta.

His impact was felt in academics as well. He was a lecturer and also the personnel appointed to handle the Fisheries section of the World Bank funded STEP-B Project of the Federal College of Education (Technical), Asaba where he had the opportunity to impact the Agriculture students of the institution with relevant aquaculture knowledge capable of making them self-reliant upon graduation. Furthermore, he has had the opportunity to serve as one of the

Fisheries Examiners and Moderators for West African Examination Council.

This book is therefore a compressed presentation of both his theoretical and field expertise. For successful fish production at all levels, this handbook is a must read

He currently lives in Canada with his family.

www.ingramcontent.com/pod-product-compliance
Lightning Source LLC
Chambersburg PA
CBHW071918070526
44583CB00016B/2043